# Miracles in Your Mouth

Be Renewed, Overcome Anxiety, Fear and Depression Through Spiritual Principals & Life-Changing Affirmations

**RAINIE HOWARD**

Also by Rainie Howard:
- ADDICTED TO PAIN
- YOU ARE ENOUGH
- WHEN GOD SENT MY HUSBAND
- UNDENIABLE BREAKTHROUGH

Rainie Howard Enterprises Publishing Agency
111 West Port Plaza, Suite 600, Maryland Heights, MO 63146

Scripture quotations are taken from the Holy Bible. All rights reserved worldwide.
Copyright © 2018 Rainie Howard Enterprises
All rights reserved, including the right to reproduce this book or portions thereof in any form whatsoever. No part of this production may be reproduced or transmitted in any form or by any means, mechanical or electronic, including photocopying or recording, or by any information storage and retrieval system, or transmitted by email without permission in writing form the publisher. While all attempts have been made to verify the information provided in this publication, neither the author nor the publisher assumes any responsibility for errors, omissions, or contrary interpretations of the subject matter herein. The views expressed are those of the author, and should not be taken as expert instruction or commands. The reader is responsible for his or her own actions. Neither the author nor the publisher assumes any responsibility or liability whatsoever on the behalf of the purchaser or reader of these materials. Any perceived slight of any individual or organization is purely unintentional. For information address Rainie Howard Enterprises, LLC www.RainieHoward.com

For information about special discounts for bulk purchases or bringing the author to your live event, please contact Rainie Howard Enterprises Sales
at 314-827-5216 or Contact@RainieHoward.com
Manufactured in the United State of America
ISBN-13: 978-1-7340155-7-7

## ACKNOWLEDGMENTS

To my Lord and Savior Jesus Christ for loving me, healing me and ordering my steps and directing my path. To my loving husband Patrick Howard and my children Bj and Aniyah Howard, your love and support has blessed me and encouraged me to never give up. To my family, friends and all of my Love Nation supporters who watch The Daily Word, thanks for sharing your stories, prayers and love. You motivate me to keep writing, keep creating and keep producing life-changing work. I love you all.

# TABLE OF CONTENTS

INTRODUCTION .................................................................. vii
CHAPTER 1: WHEN MISERY MOVES IN ................................. 11
   Stressed, Worried and Tired............................................. 16
   When Everything and Everyone Is Against You ............... 20
CHAPTER 2: OVERCOME THE THREATS AND FRETS OF
THE UNKNOWN................................................................... 29
   Stop Dreading What's Ahead............................................ 32
   Guard Your Heart from Negativity ................................... 36
CHAPTER 3: STOP CHASING WHAT GOD DIDN'T SEND .... 47
   Don't Force the Outcome; Trust God ............................... 50
   Get out of Agreement with the Enemy............................. 53
CHAPTER 4: THE DIVINE SECRET TO ENJOYING YOUR
LIFE....................................................................................... 61
   Do Your Best, and Give God the Rest .............................. 62
   Do Not Despise Small Improvements............................... 66
CHAPTER 5: YOUR STORY IS STILL BEING WRITTEN ...... 75
   The Answer to Your…Why Me, God? ............................. 78
   Your New Normal Is Often Uncomfortable..................... 79
CHAPTER 6: BE RENEWED; RECEIVE PROSPERITY AND
INCREASE ............................................................................ 89
   The Truth About Prosperity ............................................. 90
   The Reason God Gives the Power to Gain Wealth .......... 95
CONCLUSION ...................................................................... 101
ABOUT THE AUTHOR........................................................ 103

# INTRODUCTION

Your thoughts create your beliefs, your beliefs create your words, your words create your actions and your actions create your reputation and character. Finally, your reputation and character fulfills your destiny. Your destiny is your future; it's where you are headed. What you do today will determine your tomorrow. Notice how your words produce your actions. Your words have the power to direct your action. The Bible says in Proverbs 18:21 (NKJV), "Death and life are in the power of the tongue, and those who love it will eat its fruit."

There is power in your words; you have the power to speak life or death over your situation. Whatever you love saying, that's what you will experience. The Bible says, "[a]nd those who love it (speaking life or speaking death) will eat its fruit." The word fruit in this scripture is the results. To eat the fruit is to experience the life results of what you are constantly saying.

It all starts with your thinking. This is the very reason your thoughts represent who you are. Proverbs 23:7 (NKJV) says, "As [a man] thinks in his heart, so is he." Your entire future and destiny is determined by the thoughts that create your beliefs to influence your words and determine your actions.

It was the darkest season of my life. My alarm sounded off with urgency and panic as if I was in a deep sleep. It didn't wake me up, because I was awake the entire night. It was the very first night I experienced insomnia. I tried everything I could think of to help me fall asleep, and nothing worked. I took sleeping pills, tried reading myself to sleep, listened to soft instrumental music and laid with my eyes closed for hours but nothing could help me fall asleep. I tossed and turned the entire night, feeling tormented. My eyes were tired, my body was tired and my mind was tired, yet I was wide awake the entire night. Now it was time to wake up and face the day. I had to get ready for work; I had an important speaking engagement, and my energy and strength were needed. My audience was expecting a powerful message, and my weak and restless body needed to pull through.

In that season of my life, I experienced weight gain, severe exhaustion, stress, anxiety attacks, panic attacks and insomnia. Doctors had me on anti-depressants, and no medicine, human procedure or doctor could help or heal what I was encountering. There were times when I thought I was losing my mind. In the midst of the battle of my life, God helped me to never lose sight of the victory. I'm blessed to come out of all of that stronger, wiser and more confident in the power of God's spiritual principles and declaring His word in my life.

"For the word of God is living and powerful, and sharper than any two-edged sword, piercing even to the division of soul and spirit, and of joints and marrow, and is a discerner of the thoughts and intents of the heart." –Hebrews 4:12

When you speak the word of God over your life, you are releasing **Miracles in Your Mouth**.

This book is life-changing. It will inspire you to grow spiritually, emotionally and mentally. I share several stories and testimonies to encourage you to be an overcomer in any and every situation you encounter. Overcome stress, fear and anxiety. Learn spiritual secrets to living a peaceful life you enjoy, and embrace a new life of blessings and prosperity.

# CHAPTER 1

## WHEN MISERY MOVES IN

You don't understand why. Why did you have to go through that pain, why did you lose your house, why did your relationship end like that, why did you get diagnosed with that disease? Why did you lose your job, why did you go broke and why did your loved one leave so soon? The question is left unanswered, and your life is suddenly filled with nothing more than painful silence. God, why? Why me, why now and why this? When misery hits and your heart is broken, you often blame people, situations and sometimes God. You find yourself saying, "But God, I don't understand why it happened that way." I thought God was saying yes, but my life feels like a big no. It happened to me during a time when I was most energetic, hopeful, passionate, excited and determined to pursue and achieve more in my life; misery gradually moved in. I had put my all into being better, having more and accomplishing greater. My life was consumed and busy with many tasks that I strived to excel in daily. The cares and responsibilities of this world weighed me down. I had no idea I was about to enter into the battle of my life. During this season in my life, I noticed a big change. Something was different; there was a shift in my environment. I had lived in the same home for almost 10 years, but I knew it was time to move. My business had been progressing in a strategy that was working successfully, but I knew it was time to transition and innovate a new plan. My marriage had achieved over a decade of love, but I felt the tension of our relationship as we encountered the changes of our life. My husband and I were both frustrated with the unknown direction—not knowing what to do or what steps to take in this new season. The stress and tension of the shift in the atmosphere and the change in my life was making me tired spiritually, emotionally and physically. I had experienced success in the past, but it was time to change. I was entering into the in-between season; it's the season in the middle of your now and your next. It's the unknown path that bridges your present to your purpose. Misery moved in to join me in the in-between season.

When you make the decision to hold on to bitterness and resentment and choose not to forgive, misery moves in. Misery dwells with toxic emotions. When misery moves in it doesn't matter how bright and beautiful the day is; every day is cloudy and dark with misery. It doesn't matter how comfortable and gorgeous your house is; there is never any peace or joy at home with misery. Misery comes to steal, kill and destroy your hopes, dreams and life. Misery hates joy; misery never wants you to smile, laugh or enjoy life. There's no good night's rest with misery. Misery will keep you up all night long and then make you sleepy all day long. Misery has one purpose to fulfill, and that purpose is to stop you from moving forward in your life. Misery's plan is to keep you stuck in the in-between season. Misery does not want you healed and whole. Misery loves the company of depression and fear because depression and fear will keep you defeated.

I was stressed, tired and depressed. I had gained weight; I felt fatigue and exhausted daily. I started working out to gain energy and lose weight, but it only made things worse. Exercising made me feel more anxious and stressed. I started eating better, drinking more water and detoxifying my body, with little to no improvement. I sought after every professional to get advice and get help to fix my symptoms, but nothing worked. I was trying to heal the symptoms without dealing with the root issue. Someone recommended that I get medical advice from a hormone specialist; they said I was probably having hormones issues. Unfortunately, the specialist prescribed medication and supplements that led to major panic and anxiety attacks; it also caused fogginess and confusion in my mind. I even experienced extreme fatigue in my body. I ended all the medicine and kept searching for something that would solve my problems. Although the medicine ended, the toxic emotions and depression got worse. It took me a while to realize my problem wasn't medical; it was spiritual. For years I had stored the pain and resentment of my past in my heart. Those painful emotions started as seeds planted in my heart. Those seeds created roots that grew into fruit (spiritual life results). The fear, insecurity and rejection of my childhood was still active in my heart. The seeds of childhood fear grew into severe anxiety that was paralyzing me from elevating to the next level of my life. A part of me knew that I needed to release the spiritual baggage before I could enter the next level of growth in my life. I couldn't take it with me. I knew I could not survive the elevation to the next season of my life while holding on to the stress and anxiety of my past. I needed to transform my mind and change my ways. It was time to create new habits. The hurt and bitterness of my past had held me hostage in my in-between season. There were times when I felt like a prisoner in my own body. I struggled to forgive those who hurt me, and my decision to hold on to that pain left me in misery. Often times we ask God to heal our pain when God is asking us to let it go. We need to stop holding on to the resentment, release the hurt and let go of the pain. We must make the decision to move forward and leave all the bitterness behind. Not choosing forgiveness is the same as not choosing peace.

We choose to not let the hurt go, because deep down inside we want someone to pay for it. Someone else is responsible, so they must pay; we become relentless in demanding that they pay the cost. Therefore, we spend years mad and angry because of what happened to us. We willingly hold on to the past hurt all in the hope that one day we will get that apology and payback. The truth is we really want revenge. We want the people who hurt us to pay up. We fail to understand that holding on to the resentment won't bring us revenge or justice but instead that our healing comes in letting it go. When you decide to lay it down and let go of the pursuit for payback, you free yourself from the bondage of that pain.

**Stressed, Worried and Tired**

You may not have realized it, but your anxiety, fear and depression came from negative emotions that you have tucked away in your heart. These emotions come from traumatic experiences in your life that you have decided to never forget. Sometimes you relive them over and over again in your mind. That one moment is continuously showing up in your life. Although your life is different today and you are faced with different situations, your reasoning and beliefs are creating the same results because your past experience is guiding you. That toxic emotional seed that was planted years ago has grown into a fully strong tree full of fruit. It's very common for people to struggle with stress and anxiety, but many don't understand the reason they struggle with it and where it comes from.

Consider this: whatever you wake up thinking about first thing in the morning and whatever you go to bed thinking about late at night, is what has a hold on you. It's something you just can't seem to shake. It's always on your mind. What is it? Is it your relationship, your finances, your boss, your family, your job, your business, your debt or your bills? What keeps you up all night? What keeps you worried and stressed? Whatever it is, it's feeding misery. Misery eats your worries; misery is strengthened by your anxiety. Depression, anxiety and fear are like vitamins to misery.

Misery has a plan to choke the purpose and promises of God on your life. The worries of life and the deception and vanity of this world will keep you in misery. However, when you free yourself from the worries and stress of life, you make room for God to heal you and deliver you from misery.

"Still others, like seed sown among thorns, hear the word; but the worries of this life, the deceitfulness of wealth and the desires for other things come in and choke the word, making it unfruitful. Others, like seed sown on good soil, hear the word, accept it, and produce a crop—some thirty, some sixty, some a hundred times what was sown."
–Mark 4:18-20

When your heart is full of toxic emotions, it's impossible to receive, accept and produce the promises of God in your life. This is why the Bible tells us to give God all of our worries, cares and stress (1 Peter 5:7). You can't figure it out on your own; don't lose your mind trying to figure everything out. You no longer have to be bound by the cares of this world. You've been exhausted and lacking strength because you have been trying to figure everything out and fix your problems yourself. It's only by the power and strength of God that you can do all things (Philippians 4:13).

The systems of this world give false security in fame, financial wealth and glamour. It's a distraction to keep your mind off of the purpose and calling God has on your life. There's nothing wrong with having nice things; the problem is when nice things have you. The issue is when nice things have your heart, your mind and your strength. It's when you give your entire life to things. Instead you are called to give your life to God and allow Him full access to your heart, mind and strength.

"'And you shall love the Lord your God with all your heart, with all your soul, with all your mind, and with all your **strength**.'

This is the first commandment. And the second, like it, is this: 'You shall love your neighbor as yourself.' There is no other commandment greater than these." –Mark 12:30-31

We often make the mistake of filling our heart, soul and mind with the issues of life, worrying about people, places and things. They become our center of attention, and we wonder why we're so fearful, anxious and angry. It's because the cares of this life have weighted our hearts down and we have wrongly placed everything first before God.

There are so many distractions in this world pulling for your attention. There's so much pulling for your mind, but God is calling you to clear your mind of those things and seek God first.

"But seek first the kingdom of God and His righteousness, and all these things shall be added to you." – Matthew 6:33

Everything you believe you need and more shall be added unto you when you put God first.

## When Everything and Everyone Is Against You

When misery has moved in, it will feel like everything and everyone is against you. Misery wants you to believe that it's winning in your life. Understand you're in a battle. Although you are in the fight of your life, you are not battling people. Misery will deceive your mind and encourage you to complain. Your life will often feel hopeless, and everything will point to a person. The pain, hurt and disappointment of your past will point to a person. Misery will blame your parents, your cousin, your babysitter and your first-grade teacher. Misery will blame your ex, your spouse and your children. They hurt you; they mistreated you; they used you and abused you. They were against you, but they are not your enemy. The longer you decide to stay bitter and angry towards them, the longer you will dwell with misery.

We must not be surprised when people and situations come against us. It's not a shocking or strange thing happening. It's part of the process. Trials and struggles are part of the process. The Bible encourages us to rejoice in those seasons because we are partaking in the sufferings of Christ. God's glory is seen and revealed in our trial.

"Beloved, do not think it strange concerning the fiery trial which is to try you, as though some strange thing happened to you; but rejoice to the extent that you partake of Christ's sufferings, that when His glory is revealed, you may also be glad with exceeding joy." –1 Peter 4:12-13

Be careful with your heart; guard and protect your heart. People change; one day they love you and praise your works, but the very next day those same people can hate you and slander your name. Sometimes you go through trials so that you can discover the truth. The truth is revealed for you to grow in wisdom and understanding, not for you to be angry and attack them. Our battle is not against flesh and blood, but it's a spiritual battle that we fight (Ephesians 6:12). If you're struggling to forgive that person that hurt you, pray for them. Your victory comes through prayer. When you pray for them, you are weakening misery. As you pray a loving, sincere prayer for those who hurt you, misery will lose its power. Misery has no power in your choice to forgive. Misery has no power in your decision to love. You're not called to argue back and forth with that person; let go of the resentment and pray. Remember this: the only reason you are being attacked is because there is a mission in your life.

It's time to start to the process of total healing and deliverance from anxiety, depression and fear and to break up with misery. God has given us a cure for depression, fear and anxiety in His word. There are three weapons you are to use to defeat all anxiety and fear; all three weapons require you to speak. Understand that the reason it felt like depression, fear and anxiety has been winning in your life is because you have been suffering in silence. It's time for you to open up your mouth and declare the word of God. It's time to release the **Miracles in Your Mouth**.

"Be anxious for nothing, but in everything by **prayer** and **supplication**, with **thanksgiving**, let your requests be made known to God; and the peace of God, which surpasses all understanding, will guard your hearts and minds through Christ Jesus. Finally, brethren, whatever things are true, whatever things are noble, whatever things are just, whatever things are pure, whatever things are lovely, whatever things are of good report, if there is any virtue and if there is anything praiseworthy—meditate on these things. The things which you learned and received and heard and saw in me, these do, and the God of peace will be with you."

–Philippians 4:6-9

Your three weapons are prayer, supplication and thanksgiving. Understand you must speak life into that situation.

Prayer is your communication with God. Talk to God. Tell God how you feel and what you're dealing with in your life. Ask God to lead and guide you.

Supplication is your humble, transparent communication with God. It's your vulnerability and surrender to God. It's allowing yourself to be desperate for God to transform your situation. Lay out low on the floor or fall to your knees and share your truth with God.

Thanksgiving is when you show gratitude in your prayer. Thank God for all that He has done. Express your gratitude for the many blessings you have experienced. Count your blessings. The fact that you can inhale and exhale—that's something to be thankful for. There are people in hospitals that can only breathe with the help of a machine. Thank God you have life.

Write down everything that has you anxious.

_____
_____
_____
_____

Write out your prayer concerning those things.

_____
_____
_____
_____

Write out your supplication.

_____
_____
_____
_____

Write out what you're thankful for.

_____
_____
_____
_____

Now that you've answered the previous questions, answer this: What are you requesting from God?

_____

_____

_____

_____

Say the following prayer and affirmations out loud.

## Miracles in Your Mouth Prayer:

———— ༒︎ ————

Heavenly Father, let your will be done in my life. Give me everything that's needed to accomplish the purpose and calling on my life. Forgive me for the wrong that I've done, as I let go of bitterness and forgive others. Give me the fruits of the spirit, including self-control. Heal me from fear, anxiety, misery and depression. Your word says You will restore health to me and heal my wounds in Jeremiah 30:17. Thank you for healing and deliverance. In Jesus' name, amen.

## Miracles in Your Mouth Supplication, Affirmations:

God, I am tired of trying to figure this out on my own. I surrender it all to You. I release the burden. Your word says as I humble myself, pray, turn from my sin and seek Your face, You will hear me and heal my life in 2 Chronicles 7:14. I declare your word in my life today;

- The hurt and bitterness of my past is over; God has gifted me with peace and love
- I am no longer a prisoner in my own body; God has set me free. Whom Jesus set free is free indeed
- I forgive those who hurt me and I let go of the pain; I am being healed through my forgiveness
- I am no longer a member of misery's company. I refuse to dwell in misery; I am joyful, thankful and blessed
- I have made the decision to move forward in my life and leave all the bitterness behind
- As I choose to forgive, I choose to have peace
- I lay down my past pain, and I let go of the pursuit of revenge
- God has freed me from the bondage of fear

## Miracles in Your Mouth Thankful Praise:

- I am thankful for life
- I am thankful for God's grace and mercy
- I am thankful for healing
- I am thankful for wisdom and understanding
- I am thankful for divine health

**Take Action**

What one thing do you need to work on in order to enjoy your life and be free from misery?

_____
_____
_____
_____
_____

# CHAPTER 2

## OVERCOME THE THREATS AND FRETS OF THE UNKNOWN

Jamie was very driven and focused in her career. She loved being busy. She would fill her time by taking on extra projects at work, and she kept busy with the activities of her two kids after work and on the weekends. She made sure she had no time to think about her disappointments. She felt a little positive about life because she finally had some control over her seasonal depression. It came once a year around the time her mother died. During that time in her life, not only did she lose her mother but her relationship with the love of her life ended. Jamie was engaged to Brandon, and they were making big plans for their future. Jamie and Brandon had plans of purchasing a new home, and they were finalizing their dream wedding. Jamie's wedding dress was finished, their bridesmaids and groomsmen were excited, and the wedding invitations were all mailed when Jamie discovered the painful news. Carmen, Brandon's friend from college called Jamie and told her that her and Brandon had been together for a year and that she was pregnant with Brandon's child. Jamie was devastated. She felt humiliated, hurt, embarrassed and broken. For the first time in her life, she fell into a deep dark depression. Her entire life became dark. Life felt spiritually and emotionally gloomy. She lost all hope; she no longer had any energy or excitement for life. Every part of her being was weak and stricken with sorrow. On the outside she did everything she could to look strong and happy. Although she would smile on the outside, she was crying on the inside. She dressed up, wore make-up and looked beautiful on the outside, but on the inside she was bitter, angry and depressed.

Instead of being happy and positive about life, she became jealous, prideful and revengeful. How could

Brandon cheat on me with her? I am a better woman. I did everything to keep him happy, and he treated me like I meant nothing.

Jamie made the decision to be tough and to never allow anyone else close to her heart. She was done with relationships. She was so hurt and resentful that she vowed to never get married and never trust another man. In her mind life was too painful and she would rather avoid it all by keeping busy. Unfortunately, her bitterness and anger made her feel worse than when she first heard the devastating news. The depression got deeper and darker. Each day she struggled with feeling worse and worse. Whenever her friends would bring up Brandon in conversation, Jamie would get so upset, and an uncontrollable rage would rise up out of her. She would talk about how much she hated him and never wanted anything to do with him. Jamie was angry, but she was also confused because every time someone brought up Brandon she would cry. Why am I crying over him? I don't love him anymore; it's been years, and I'm over him, so why am I still crying over that loser?

What Jamie didn't realize was that she was in a secret inner war. She was fighting a spiritual battle in her mind, and that battle started from toxic emotions in her heart. She hated being bored or being alone, because whenever she had time to herself she would think about her mother's death and how Brandon broke her heart. She tried her best to avoid thinking about it, but it was always there leading her decisions. It affected her relationship with her children. She had lost all patience and often uncontrollably yelled at her kids for their mistakes. She was very protective of them and would never allow them to go with friends unless they were under her supervision.

**Stop Dreading What's Ahead**

Jamie did not enjoy life. She was always fearful and worried. She started to see life differently. She began only seeing the bad in life. It was as if she looked at life through a filter of pain. She saw pain and misery in everything. Jamie began to struggle with anxiety. Instead of focusing on what happened in her past, she started worrying about what could happen in her future. Her joy was robbed by the threats and frets of the unknown. She had fooled herself into thinking she was over her past, because she had learned how to keep busy and distract herself, but she was tormented by the possibilities of what could happen in her future. She was threatened by the unknown. She couldn't enjoy her promotion at work, because she was threatened by the possibility of getting laid off. She couldn't really enjoy her moments with her children, because she was constantly distracted by the school shootings she heard about on the news. The thoughts of losing her children tormented her every time they enjoyed special moments together. Those thoughts took her out of the moment and into an imagination of a future filled with fear and heartache. Those thoughts would steal her peace and joy. Although Jamie's life was full of blessings from her children and career, she couldn't enjoy her life. You may be like Jamie—you have a blessed life but struggle to enjoy it.

"The thief does not come except to steal, and to kill, and to destroy. I have come that they may have life, and that they may have it more abundantly." –John 10:10

The enemy is a thief; he wants to rob you of enjoying your life. He does this through threats. It's the threats of the possibility of pain. The enemy wants to steal, kill and destroy any hopes of your future by stealing the present moment through threats and lies about the unknown. The enemy doesn't have the power to do anything he is threatening you with if you don't give him the power. You give him the power by agreeing with him and opening the door to fear. You must denounce the threats that torment your mind with the word of God.

Peace is the treasure that the enemy attacks. Jamie had to learn how to protect her peace and value it. The enemy will use anything he can to steal, kill and destroy your peace. Jamie didn't love anyone like she loved her children. They were all she had in this world. Her children were the motivation that kept her working hard, and they were her reason for not ending her life after having suicidal thoughts. As much as she loved them, she couldn't enjoy them, because of the fear of losing them. This is the reason the Bible tells us to not worry about anything. If you worry and become anxious, the enemy uses that open door of fear and anxiety to attack what you're worried about. Jamie needed to heal her heart from the pain of losing her mother and the bitterness of losing her relationship with Brandon. Her past pain and bitterness was stealing the peace and joy in her present moments of life.

When you dread what's ahead, it steals the peace and blessings of your now moment. Instead of enjoying your life now, you're worried about the threats of your tomorrow. When you begin to understand that God is with you wherever you go, you won't have to worry about what tomorrow brings, because God will never leave you nor forsake you. Years ago I experience a panic attack. It came out of nowhere. I had never experienced anything like that before, and it shook me up. I went to the hospital trying to understand what was going on with me. I was fearful of my life. After having that panic attack, I struggled with the fear of driving on the highway, because I was dreading having another panic attack. I thank God for total healing and deliverance; however, the enemy often tried to use my mind and emotions to attack my faith. The enemy threw arrows of doubt. He would say, "You're not healed; you still don't feel normal. Something is wrong with you; something bad is going to happen, so get ready." I learned how to fight his lies and deception with my faith (1 Timothy 6:12). Instead of receiving the fearful thoughts, I stood on my faith and trust in what God says about me. God would say, "I'm with you; I'm protecting you. I will never leave you. Your life is in my hands; trust Me." I used the word of God and my faith as my weapons.

**Guard Your Heart from Negativity**

"In addition to all this, take up the shield of faith, with which you can extinguish all the flaming arrows of the evil one." –Ephesians 6:16

The flaming arrows that the enemy tries to attack you with are doubt, unbelief in God, fear, anxiety and hatred and many others. You are to fight back with your faith. The Bible talks about the shield of faith. It is your protection from the enemy. I've learned how to put all my trust in the Lord. When thoughts, feelings and invisible flaming arrows of doubt, fear and anxiety try to come to me, I don't allow them to enter my heart. I fight back with my faith and trust in God. I don't trust my feelings, emotions and thoughts; I trust God.

"Trust in the LORD with all your heart and lean not on your own understanding; in all your ways submit to him, and he will make your paths straight." –Proverbs 3:5-6

I don't trust in my own understanding; I trust in the Lord. I submit all my ways, thoughts and feelings to God. I overcome all things through my faith and trust in the Lord. My faith is one of the weapons I use to win the spiritual battle of my life.

Jamie was trying to win her spiritual battle by staying busy and trying to ignore what was tormenting her daily. She started dreading relationships because of the pain and hurt she encountered with Brandon. She didn't realize that Brandon was not her enemy. She spent too much time and energy fighting the wrong way. She needed to fight with love, forgiveness and faith. She decided to give her life to Jesus and receive the Holy Spirit. She asked God to forgive her of her bitterness, hatred and jealousy. She released the resentment she had in her heart towards Brandon and decided to forgive him. She was immediately healed from depression and fear. Jamie is no longer bound by the weight of anxiety, and she is enjoying her life free from all toxic emotions.

Here's an excerpt about toxic emotions from my book, **You Are Enough: Overcoming People Pleasing And Emotionally Unavailable Relationships**:

Fighting people hurts you the most. You destroy your toxic emotional roots through spiritual attacks (such as prayer and forgiveness), not by hurting others. You can't free yourself through fighting with your ex or saying hateful words to someone who abused you. Remember, your emotional roots are about you, not other people, and they are intangible. It's important that you understand that negative emotions are not physical things, but they are spiritual things that have the power to manifest physical things, and that is why they must be addressed. Everything you see in the physical ream came from a thought in the spiritual ream. We all know a thought can't be physically seen it is first unseen in the spiritual ream. The computer I'm currently typing on came from the thoughts of a computer engineer, the chair I'm sitting in came from the mind of a furniture designer and the home I live in came from the thoughts and creativity of an architect. Your life is a physical manifestation of your thoughts, beliefs, dreams and expectations. Everything you store in the spiritual ream of your mind creates the physically manifested results of your life.

You may be thinking, "But I didn't create the person who mistreated and hurt me." That is true, and sometimes innocent victims are wrongfully mistreated and had nothing to do with their abuser's choices. Each person has a free will and we are not in control of the actions of others. But we are in control of what we allow ourselves to believe, think and expect. This is why two people can both experience the same abuse, neglect and rejection from an abusive relationship but respond differently from each other and experience different results in their lives. One person decides to forgive the person who hurt them, release the pain and live a peaceful, thankful life. The other person decides to hold on to the pain, anger and resentment and live a chaotic, drama-filled life. Although they both had the same painful experiences, both ended up with very different life results because of the individual emotions rooted in them.

This is why it's so important to get rid of the toxic emotional roots in your life. Matthew 3:10 talks about cutting them down and destroying them. "Already now the ax is applied to the root of the trees. Therefore every tree not producing good fruit is cut down and thrown into the fire." Remember that your thoughts create your words, your words create your actions, your actions create your habits and your habits create your character. What's in you comes out. When we are rooted in bitterness and hatred, we produce a life of bitter, hateful fruit, and this fruit is our character. Our character is a reflection of what's inside of us. Do you have trouble controlling your temper? Do you have a tendency to complain and feel ungrateful? It's important to analyze what's rooted in you.

There was a season in my life when God had to perform soul surgery on me. I had never known or heard about soul surgery until receiving revelation while journaling. God revealed to me that I was going to go through a process of soul surgery that year.

Fear, disappointment and the pain of my past were hurting my soul, and I had no idea how much it was damaging my life. Surgery isn't fun or appealing but it's often necessary to treat injuries and disorders. It was a process of being open, getting to the roots of past hurt, exposing them and bringing it all to surface. The childhood fear, the sadness, unforgiving ways and insecurity tried to take me down, but God patiently waited for me to surrender it all to Him. God wanted to take it out through soul surgery, but I was trying to feel better while keeping it. I was trying to fix it on my own, so I tried everything else. I went to a therapist, and she could not help me; then my doctor prescribed antidepressants, and that made me feel worse. Finally, I decided to quiet my mind and follow the Holy Spirit; I listened carefully for His guidance, and He led me to total deliverance. Like His word says, He created in me a clean heart and renewed a right spirit within me (Psalm 51:10). After my soul surgery I went through the healing and recovery process. God's wisdom taught me how to protect my heart and use discernment in my relationships. That soul surgery was painful but purposeful. It prepared me for greater. Understand that the struggle you encounter is necessary for the strength required in your future.

Say the following prayer and affirmations out loud.

## Miracles in Your Mouth Prayer:

———— ✦✧✦✧ ————

Heavenly Father, my life is in your hands. Help me to stop dreading my future and remove all toxic emotions that weigh me down. I release bitterness and resentment, and I receive your love and grace. Help me to guard my heart and trust you with all of my heart. Your word says You are with me wherever I go (Joshua 1:9). Thank you for healing and deliverance. In Jesus' name, amen.

## Miracles in Your Mouth Supplication, Affirmations:

God, I surrender the dread and the fear of the unknown to You. My future is in your hands. I am not longer worried about what tomorrow may bring. I know that You are ordering my steps and directing my path. Have Your way in my life, Jesus. I declare your word in my life today;

- God is strengthening me daily in every area of my life
- I don't worry about anything; instead I pray about everything, and God directs my path
- I trust in the Lord with all of my heart
- I acknowledge God in everything I do
- I'm excited about my future; God has great plans for me
- God is blessing me exceedingly, abundantly above everything I can ask or think of
- I trust God with all of the uncertainty and unknown answers of my life
- God has given me peace, which surpasses all understanding

## Miracles in your Mouth Thankful Praise:

———— ❧❦❧ ————

- I am thankful for peace of mind
- I am thankful for God's forgiveness
- I am thankful for the healing of my past
- I am thankful for each and every day of my life
- I am thankful for my sanity

**Take Action:**

What one thing do you need to stop dreading about your future?

_____
_____
_____
_____
_____

# CHAPTER 3

# STOP CHASING WHAT GOD DIDN'T SEND

I was frustrated, discouraged and confused. To be honest I was a bit upset with God. I had never felt so disappointed. How do you go from hopefully expecting one of the biggest financial blessings in your life to losing it all, your house and your savings? How do you go from believing that God is about to open up the windows of Heaven and pour out the blessing of your life to feeling defeated and forsaken? It felt like the enemy was laughing in my face, and all I could do was cry out, "Why, God, I just don't understand why?"

It was early spring when my husband and I decided to sell our home and relocate our family. After putting the house on the market, it sold in four days with an offer so good we couldn't refuse. We were expecting to profit in an amount much greater than the average American annual salary. This was big for our family; we could pay down debt, build up our credit score, increase savings and reinvest in new property in a more progressive neighborhood. In my vision our future looked amazing. The deal was going great. Because our home sold so fast, we decided to secure a temporary lease of an apartment while we built a new home. We signed the lease, packed up, hired movers and moved in to a temporary apartment.

Our closing day was a week away, and in the middle of moving furniture into the apartment, we receive a phone call from our real estate agent. She sounded worried as she said, "Something is not right; the title company is saying that there is another mortgage on your home that needs to be paid at closing. Once it's paid you will need to bring money to closing to pay the remainder amount." I immediately said, "Oh no, there must be a mistake; there is no extra mortgage on our home. We can prove it."

We spent the following month hiring lawyers, submitting documents and fighting banks to prove we never agreed to another mortgage on our home. Unfortunately, we discovered that after modifying our home years prior to selling it, there was a silent HUD mortgage (that we never knew of) added to our mortgage. We decided to sell the house and pay the remainder balance at closing. The entire process was disappointing, but the entire time God encouraged me to not be discouraged. The money it cost to sell our house, hire lawyers and pay closing fees and the down payment to build a new house left us with much less than we started.

For some reason we were still trying to force our original plan to build a new house in the neighborhood we desired. We were so committed to our vision that we became stubborn to make it happen. Although the doors of our vision were closed, we kept trying to force them open. The more I prayed that God would open the doors to my own will, the more I saw them close. Years ago I used to thank God for the open doors, but now after going through what I went through I thank Him also for the doors that are closed. Back when I was going through the disappointment of the closed doors, I didn't realize that those closed doors were for my protection. Back then I couldn't understand that losing the profit from the house and losing the down payment from building a new house and not having either house was God's way of ordering my steps and directing my path (Psalm 37:23).

## Don't Force the Outcome; Trust God

When the trial was new, I couldn't understand why it was necessary. I didn't understand that you have to humble yourself before God will exalt you (1 Peter 5:6). I needed to get my heart right. I was seeking fulfillment from a house and bank account, and God was showing me that He is the only fulfillment. I was chasing a vision that God never sent. I was chasing my own will and failing to surrender my will to God's purpose for my life. In my vision I thought getting approved for a new loan to finance a new house was a blessing, but God was saying, "Stop limiting yourself; I'm preparing you for ownership." He told me, "I'm preparing you to be debt-free and never owe no man (bank, loan or credit card company) anything but love" (Romans 13:8). I didn't realize I was limiting God by trying to force my vision. I was chasing what God didn't send. The truth was that I wasn't ready for the amount of money we expected to profit from selling our house. That money would have been used to accumulate more debt.

God was leading us to be transformed. It was time for me to renew my mind.

"And be not conformed to this world: but be ye transformed by the renewing of your mind, that ye may prove what is that good, and acceptable, and perfect, will of God." –Romans 12:2

I was so conformed to buying what I desired, and if I couldn't afford it, I would finance it. Financing things and getting them on credit gave me a false belief that I could afford it. That mindset is deceiving; you believe you earned it and even own it, but you are under contract for 15-30 years to pay a bank for it. I begin to transform my mind so that I could prove God's good, acceptable and perfect will for my life. God is calling us to be wise stewards over all that He has given us, our families, finances and future. God blesses us so that we can be a blessing. We are called to advance the kingdom of God and be lenders not borrowers.

"The LORD will open to you His good treasure, the heavens, to give the rain to your land in its season, and to bless all the work of your hand. You shall lend to many nations, but you shall not borrow. And the LORD will make you the head and not the tail; you shall be above only, and not be beneath, if you heed the commandments of the LORD your God, which I command you today, and are careful to observe them." –Deuteronomy 28:12-13

You were created for a specific purpose. God has a plan for your life. It's important that you surrender your plan to God. What have you been chasing that God didn't send? Are you seeking fulfillment in a career, relationship or a new house? God is more than enough. You have a vision for that relationship, and you see it going in a certain direction, but you realize later that what you envision isn't your reality. You've been expecting things to be a certain way because you were trying to control the outcome. Surrender that vision to God. Ask God to write the vision, order your steps and direct your path. Instead of trying to force a relationship, pray and surrender it to God. If they left they weren't meant to stay. Bless them and keep seeking God.

## Get out of Agreement with the Enemy

My mind was too wrapped up in the cares of this world (my house, my money and other worldly possessions), and it was causing stress, anxiety and fear. One morning I was laying in the bed, praying and reading the following scripture.

"Still others, like seed sown among thorns, hear the word; but the worries of this life, the deceitfulness of wealth and the desires for other things come in and choke the word, making it unfruitful." –Mark 4:18-19

After reading that scripture while lying in my bed, I said, "God, I no longer want anything if it's not from you. I don't want money, success, houses or fame if it's not from you." After saying those words out loud, something miraculous happened. The severe anxiety pressure that I felt for over a year weighing my chest down lifted. That spirit of anxiety left. I've been totally healed and free since. I had to get out of agreement with the enemy. The enemy will tempt you with your fleshy desires. I fell for his lies and started agreeing with the pursuit of houses, money and success, without yielding to God's will. Those things consumed my mind. They became burdensome to my life. The obsessive pursuits were stressful. Make sure that you are believing, trusting and agreeing with God. Eve didn't sin in the garden of Eden until she believed, trusted and agreed with the serpent (Genesis 3:1-7). Saying "trust God" may sound cliché, but did you know you can love God, worship God and believe in God but still not trust God. Trusting God requires you to surrender it all and rely on Him alone. Trust God not your pay check, trust God not your education, trust God not your past experience.

"Trust in the LORD with all your heart, and lean not on your own understanding; In all your ways acknowledge Him, and He shall direct your paths." –Proverbs 3:5-6

When you believe God you are accepting His word, His plan and works as truth. You are making up your mind that everything God is saying and doing in your life is truth and that you trust and rely on Him alone. When you connect your trust and your belief together, the results are your agreement. Agreeing with God means you have the same opinion as God. That's powerful. When you start agreeing with God, you join Him, walking together in partnership.

"What agreement has the temple of God with idols? For we are the temple of the living God; as God said, 'I will make my dwelling among them and walk among them, and I will be their God, and they shall be my people.'" –2 Corinthians 6:16

Because agreeing with God can transform your life for the better, you can imagine how agreeing with the enemy can cause turmoil. Don't get me wrong—agreeing with the enemy isn't something obvious. It can be subtle and deceptive. You may not realize it, but when you confess things with your mouth, you are guiding your future. Years ago I used to always say, "I'm so tired. I can't do all that; it's too much; I don't have friends; no one understands me." The more I would say those things, the more I would receive those things. I was always tired, always limited in my energy, had a hard time finding genuine friends and always felt like no one understood me. I was saying exactly what the enemy wanted me to say; I didn't know it, but I was in agreement with the enemy.

"Death and life are in the power of the tongue, And those who love it will eat its fruit." –Proverbs 18:21

"For 'Whoever desires to love life and see good days, let him keep his tongue from evil and his lips from speaking deceit;'" –1 Peter 3:10

When you speak negativity you attract negativity, and you experience and live a life filled with negative outcomes. You must become determined to get out of agreement with the enemy. Speak as if you are already healed, energetic, blessed and surrounded by good friends and family who love, care and understand you.

"(As it is written, I have made thee a father of many nations,) before him whom he believed, even God, who quickeneth the dead and calleth those things which be not, as though they were." –Romans 4:17

You need to talk like you're blessed, even when your current situation doesn't look like it. You are to walk by faith and not by sight (2 Corinthians 5:7).

Say the following prayer and affirmations out loud.

## Miracles in Your Mouth Prayer:

Heavenly Father, I let go of chasing things you didn't send. I will no longer try to force the outcome. I get out of agreement with the enemy. I choose to trust, believe and agree with you, God. Let your will be done in my life. I don't want it if it didn't come from you, God. Help me to speak words of life and strength. Let the words of my mouth and the meditation of my heart be acceptable to you, God (Psalm 19:14). Thank you for total healing and deliverance. In Jesus' name, amen.

## Miracles in Your Mouth Supplication, Affirmations:

God, I let go of my selfish will and negative ways. I surrender it all to you. I turn from my negative habits, and I join together in partnership and complete agreement with you. I declare your word in my life today;

- I am encouraged and optimistic
- I am victorious and hopeful
- I thank God for open doors of new opportunity
- I thank God for closed doors of protection

- I humble myself, and God exalts me in due season
- God is blessing me to be a lender and not a borrower
- I am called to be debt free; I owe no one anything but love
- God is blessing the work of my hands
- I am the head and not the tail; I am above and not beneath
- God created me for a special purpose
- God has great plans for my life
- I trust in the Lord with all my heart
- God is directing my path
- I speak the positivity I want to see as if it already exists

**Miracles in Your Mouth Thankful Praise:**

- I am thankful for this present moment
- I am thankful for God's grace
- I am thankful for life
- I am thankful for my family and friends
- I am thankful for my relationship with God

**Take Action:**

What one thing do you need to stop dreading about your future?

_____

_____

_____

_____

_____

## CHAPTER 4

## THE DIVINE SECRET TO ENJOYING YOUR LIFE

As a young girl, I grew up with a lot of responsibility. I am the oldest sibling of four, and I was responsible for cleaning the house, cooking and helping to care for my sibling, as my mom worked two jobs to take care of us. I saw the struggles and sacrifices she made as motivation to work hard, struggle and sacrifice even when I didn't have to. I didn't know how important balance was; hard work, struggle and sacrifice became my habits. At age 15 I got my first job, and I worked throughout high school and college. Unfortunately, I started to believe that my performance gave me value. I strived hard and worked while maintaining a 4.0 in college. I felt valuable from my accomplishments. After getting a bachelor's and master's degree with top grades, I felt like I was proving to myself and to others that I was valuable, but still that wasn't enough. I wanted more recognition and acceptance, so I worked hard, achieving everything I could in my career. In addition to being performance-driven, I struggled with being a perfectionist. Now you can only image how difficult it could be trying to enjoy life while striving to outperform the perfect image in your mind. For years I thought the pressures and anxiety I felt came from my encounters with others and the day-to-day struggles of life. I was wrong. Much of my pressures, anxiety and fear was brought on by me. I volunteered to carry heavy burdens that I created. I pushed myself to do more, be more and work hard for more. I made it difficult to enjoy my present moments, because I was so distracted by meeting the deadlines of my future. I pressured myself.

**Do Your Best, and Give God the Rest**

It's like painting a picture of the perfect image you desire for your life, then forcing the reality of life to look like the picture you've painted. That is impossible. Now imagine thinking that way and knowing it's impossible but believing God is going to make it happen. We know that with God all things are possible, but we must be careful to not try to control God's hand. Let God be God. We must learn to be still and know He alone is God (Psalm 46:10). It's the process of surrender.

Instead of controlling your plan and forcing the outcome, surrender. Don't be discouraged when things don't go as you plan. Do your best and don't take life results personally. The outcome is not your fault. You can't control everything; you live in an imperfect world, so stop striving for perfection. Do your best, and give God the rest. You need to stop stressing over the things you can't control. In life we are called to plant and water seeds, and God brings the harvest.

"Who then is Paul, and who is Apollos, but ministers through whom you believed, as the Lord gave to each one? I planted, Apollos watered, but God gave the increase. So then neither he who plants is anything, nor he who waters, but God who gives the increase. Now he who plants and he who waters are one, and each one will receive his own reward according to his own labor." –1 Corinthians 3:5-8

You can't control the results; all you can do is be a good steward and trust God with the outcome. Let go of your plans and surrender your will to God. As you let go and wait on God, He will give you the strategies and direct your path in all your pursuits.

When you make the decision to free yourself from performance and perfectionism, that heavy burden you've been carrying will release. It feels amazing, and you will begin to experience His peace which surpasses all understanding.

I had to let go of being performance driven and let go of my need to be perfect. I've learned to diligently plant and water seeds as God leads and give Him the glory for the results. The increase has nothing to do with me and how well I perform, but the harvest is from the Lord. The systems of this world celebrate performance-driven people. Unfortunately, those same people are overworked, underpaid and severely stressed. They overperform to increase sales and profits for big corporations, and they're often left tired and unhappy. Many performance-driven people don't even know how to relax on vacation and enjoy life. Many of them don't take vacations, because they prefer to work, or they work while on vacation. It's a man-made systematic way of thinking that didn't come from God. God never created us for that kind of pressure.

"Do not overwork to be rich; because of your own understanding, cease! Will you set your eyes on that which is not? For riches certainly make themselves wings; They fly away like an eagle toward heaven." –Proverbs 23:4-5

We live in a "Hollywood-centered culture," and because of social media and reality TV, we are exposed to the overworked, demanding lifestyles of the rich and famous. We have normalized a performance-driven society. Our children are raising themselves and our marriages are failing because we're too busy and when we are home we're too tired to really connect. Many of us Christians have adopted the same habits while believing it's for God. God never called us to carry that performance-driven burden.

"Come to Me, all you who labor and are heavy laden, and I will give you rest. Take My yoke upon you and learn from Me, for I am gentle and lowly in heart, and you will find rest for your souls. For My yoke is easy and My burden is light." –Matthew 11:28-30

God's burden is light, not stressful, exhausting and brutal. We are effective as we live balanced lives. Work and play; when you complete long tiring projects, take time for long, relaxing vacations. Each day create boundaries for work and relaxation; your work time should never spill over into your family time. You can't be everything to everyone. People who struggle with being performance-driven try to figure out every solution, answer the call to every need and be the hero every day. When do you get a break? When is your day off? When can you relax when you're fixing everything every day? Remember, it's only one you. Stop trying to be everything to everyone. You are not the savior of the world; rest in your Lord and Savior Jesus Christ.

**Do Not Despise Small Improvements**

For years I struggled with being a people pleaser. There were many times when someone would ask me to do something that I really didn't want to do, but I would force myself to say yes and take on the burden. I worried about what people would think about me if I said no. I often felt guilty if I couldn't come through for others when they asked. Thank God I'm now free from people pleasing. I've learned that I'm called to do everything I do as unto God and not people (Ephesians 6:7). If God is ok with my no, then that's all that matters. I used to think, "But what if they're mad at me, and what will they think about me if I said, 'No'?" That thinking held me hostage for years. Once I begin to fix my mind on Jesus and honoring Him in everything I do, it didn't matter what people thought about me. I live for Jesus; I'm called to do everything as if I'm serving Him and not people.

God never gives you more than you can bear, but you may give yourself more than you can bear, and often times other people will give you more than you can bear. When it comes from God, it comes with grace. God gives us the grace to persevere and endure everything He gives us. When you put more on your plate than you can handle, you'll be left with many unfinished assignments, or you'll be overwhelmed, stressed and anxious, trying to do what you were never called to do.

How do you enjoy life when everything you pursue and every opportunity you move towards seems to fail? How do you enjoy life when the people you love hurt you the most?

How do you enjoy life when you've tried your best but most of your efforts become failures? When life gets tough it's very difficult to enjoy. My life seemed to be moving at a much slower pace than some of my peers. I compared my progress with the success and progression of others. Why wasn't my business moving as fast as the other leaders in the industry? Why wasn't I getting the recognition and attention as other women in my community?

Have you ever questioned why your life seemed to be moving slow with only small improvements?

Samantha was so frustrated with the progression of her life. She kept wondering, "Why am I always the bridesmaid and never the bride, and why can't I find a job that pays me enough so that I don't have to live paycheck to paycheck? Why does it seem like everyone else has a beautiful house and brand-new car but I've had my same home and car for eleven years?" Samantha was discontent with her life. The grass always looked greener on the other side, and she couldn't enjoy what God was doing in her life.

When you ignore the small improvement of your life and fail to count your blessings, you attract more reasons to not enjoy your life and be ungrateful.

Here's an excerpt about taking small diligent steps from my book, **Undeniable Breakthrough: Transform Your Life And Defeat Everything That's Blocking Your Blessings**:

"The truth is you will be blessed when you are faithful to consistently do what God has called you to do. Your breakthrough will manifest after you've completed the tests and trials while trusting God and seeking Him daily. The bible says;

"Do you see a man diligent in his work? He shall stand before kings." –Proverbs 22:29

This means that no matter where you are currently in your life, if you are faithful and diligent in following the plan of God (which will be small consistent steps that lead to bigger blessings), you will be promoted and presented before great people.

Often when God has given us an assignment or vision, we think of the fastest way to accomplish it; however, when it comes to the things of God, there's always a process. We can see the evidence in nature. When an apple seed is planted in the ground, it takes 2-5 years until the tree bears any fruit. After conceiving a baby, there's a nine month process that every mother has to endure in order to give birth to that child. Therefore, why do we expect our prayers to be answered immediately and why do we expect God to trust us with stewardship over life responsibilities we didn't work for?

Instant gratification is a common trait that most people have, being consistently diligent in the pursuit of a goal is as rare as a ten-carat diamond.

"The plans of the diligent leads surely to advantage."-Proverbs 21:5"

As you become faithful with little God will elevate you to be a leader over more (Matthew 25:23). It's important that you don't rush the process. Be patient and consistent in everything God has called you to.

Say the following prayer and affirmations out loud.

## Miracles in Your Mouth Prayer:

———— ❧☙ ————

Heavenly Father, I let go of the performance-driven mindset. I understand that my value and salvation don't come from my performance, but through grace by faith I am made righteous in Christ Jesus. I am letting go of perfectionism. I will no longer be controlled by the pressures of outperforming the perfect images in my mind. I choose to rest in you, God. I'm thankful for the small improvements, and I will diligently take the small, necessary steps to fulfill the purpose and calling on my life. Thank you for total healing and deliverance. In Jesus' name, amen.

## Miracles in Your Mouth Supplication, Affirmations:

God, I surrender my imperfection and faults to you. Have your way in me. I'm dedicated to being faithful with what You have given me and diligently seek your will for my life. I declare your word in my life today;

- My value and worth is in Jesus; I am a child of the King of Kings
- I enjoy my life; each day is a day that God has made, and I rejoice and I'm glad in it

- I do my best and give God the rest

- As a good steward I trust God with the outcome

- I surrender to God's will, and He gives me the strategies, and He directs my path

- When I complete long, challenging projects, I take time for long, relaxing vacations

- Everything I do is unto God; I'm not called to be a people pleaser

- As I'm faithful with little, God is elevating me for greater

- I am faithful and diligent in everything God has called me to

**Miracles in Your Mouth Thankful Praise:**

- I am thankful for my Lord and Savior Jesus Christ
- I am thankful for each and every day of my life
- I am thankful God is ordering my steps
- I am thankful for times of relaxation
- I am thankful for the peace of God

**Take Action:**

What one thing do you need to diligently do?

_____

_____

_____

_____

_____

## CHAPTER 5

## YOUR STORY IS STILL BEING WRITTEN

One night I was experiencing a lot of pressure and tension in my body. Earlier in this day I was really exhausted and fatigued. I was so tired, but no matter what I did, I couldn't sleep. I could tell I was struggling with insomnia. I prayed and cried out to God for hours to take this tension away so that I could get some rest and go to sleep. After praying I could still feel the pressure, but I laid down and fell asleep. I woke up a couple hours later, and I was tested with a very negative thought from the enemy saying, "God still didn't remove that tension; it's still there." The enemy was trying to turn me away from God, but instead of me becoming angry and questioning God, I started thanking God for being with me and giving me a little rest. I told God I trusted Him with my situation and I knew He was working it out for my good. Several days went by, and each day God would show me things I needed to do to get better. I started taking vitamins and supplements that energized me during the day. I discovered my body was deficient of several vitamins, and the deficiency cause severe exhaustion. I also discovered that I wasn't drinking enough water, and it was causing dry skin and dandruff. I start learning more about foods I needed to eat, and finally I discovered that I was dealing with high stress hormones. My demanding work schedule and project deadlines were increasing my stress hormones. I started changing my schedule and making more time to rest and exercise. I could feel the huge difference in my body after implementing vitamins and supplements, drinking more water and exercising. The anxiety, exhaustion and insomnia and dry skin gradually went away. God reminded me that prior to experiencing all the tension and stress, I had been praying for four weeks that God would teach me how to eat, drink and exercise according to my body. I no longer wanted to follow the latest diet program or popular fitness plan; I wanted God's special plan for my life. God reminded me of my prayer, and He also reminded me that He told me that He would give me the grace to live a more balanced life. It all made sense in that moment. The insomnia, exhaustion, fatigue and stress were working together for my good. If God would have healed me completely that first night I prayed, I would have never learned about my body's deficiencies and the important supplements I needed. I would have never learned the major benefits exercise has on my energy and stress hormones. If God would have just healed me that night, I would not have learned that I needed to remove several things from my demanding work schedule and make more time for rest and vacations. That night of struggle worked together for my good. I didn't realize it at the time, but God was answering my prayers in my pain.

No matter what you're dealing with, give it to God. Don't worry about it; don't become angry because you don't understand it. Trust God to work it out for your good.

"And we know that all things work together for good to those who love God, to those who are the called according to His purpose." –Romans 8:28

I'm not sure what you're currently struggling with in your life right now, but no matter what it is, understand that God is faithful to work it out. Trust in the Lord with all your heart. Give it to God and acknowledge Him in everything you do, and I'm a living witness that He will direct your path. You may not know what decision to make or which way to go, but trust God to order your steps and direct your path. God will never let you down. Even when your life looks like God has forgotten about you, keep trusting Him. Understand that our ways are not His ways and our thoughts are not His thoughts.

**The Answer to Your…Why Me, God?**

Have you ever asked the question, "Why Me, God?" Why did this happen and why now? I want to encourage you to understand that your situation of struggle serves a purpose to build your strength. You may not understand it now, but as you continue to trust God, in due time you'll see that God has been working it all out for your good. You may not understand why things didn't work out the way you envisioned after praying. What looks like a setback is really a setup for you to be more than a conqueror through Christ.

You often get upset when the trials of life come and it seems like God isn't with you. The enemy uses your weak moment to try to deceive you into thinking evil is winning. The enemy wants you to believe that there's no hope, and he even wants you to doubt God. When you start doubting God and believing there's no hope, you invite many dark emotions into your heart. Anger, resentment and bitterness will move into your heart when you allow the challenges of life to cause you to give up your faith and trust in the Lord.

It's important that you understand that life is constantly changing. Life is changing by the moment. Your mind and reasoning is no longer the same as it was ten years ago. Whatever you're dealing with right now will have an end to it, and things will change. Often times we desire change for the good; we want things to change for the better. But how do you handle change when it doesn't look or feel good? How do you deal with change when things change for the worse? The changes of life that occur when a relationship has ended or a career has failed aren't as encouraging as the changes of falling in love and being promoted in your job. Your life in this season is changing. Instead of being fearful and avoiding the change, you should get comfortable and embrace life changes as normal. Don't get discouraged by your current situation; your story is still being written.

**Your New Normal Is Often Uncomfortable**

Everything in my life moved rapidly fast. There were so many changes in such a short time that I had a difficult time accepting it all. I had published four books in two years, relocated our entire family, grown a business, produced a show and hosted over eight conferences. On top of all of that, my relationships changed; some ended and others renewed. I felt lonelier and sometimes misunderstood. At times I felt like I was surrounded by so many blessings of elevation and change along with disappointments and discouragements. I couldn't understand why the people of TV and social media seemed to have great days every day, and I was struggling to survive.

I didn't realize that they also had struggles; they just didn't post about them. One of my close friendships ended during this time. We had been friends since high school. We would talk on the phone every day, exercise together and help each other overcome the challenges of life. I had a feeling our season of friendship was coming to an end. She began to act possessive and jealous of other relationships I had. She would even get upset when I spent time with other friends. As much as I enjoyed our relationship, it became toxic. Instead of feeling energized and happy when she called, I felt drained. I noticed my reaction to her phone calls and how it started to feel like pressure and work. We were changing, life was transitioning and we needed to embrace the change. During your season of change, you may feel lonely. The truth is you're not lonely; God is separating you from people who can't go with you to the next level. If they're not willing to grow with you, then they can't go with you into the new season of life. Some relationships are only for a season. As you embrace the new level of your life, God will connect you with new relationships. Don't allow what's familiar to mess up what's better. Your past may look attractive, but it's attacking your future. Move forward in what God is doing in the now season of your life. We often get distracted by what's familiar. What's familiar feels safe because it's what we're used to. It's our comfort zone. It's the very reason most people struggle to end toxic relationships; they are familiar. We fear loneliness and would rather suffer in our familiar mess than to soar in the future of change.

Here's an excerpt about the fear of loneliness from my book, **Addicted To Pain: Renew Your Mind And Heal Your Spirit From A Toxic Relationship In 30 Days**:

> "Relationships are like glass. Sometimes it's better to leave one broken than hurt yourself trying to put it back together." (Anonymous)

Most people are afraid to end a toxic relationship because they fear loneliness. To be honest, in the beginning of the breakup, there will be times when you will feel alone. It may not even matter if you're in a room full of people. You may be with friends and family and still feel alone. It's normal to stay up all night crying and asking God why. Maybe you're anticipating these feelings because you've felt in the past like you couldn't go on without your ex. Losing him may have left a sharp pain in your heart that's so strong you wonder if it will ever go away. I want you to know that you're not alone. You will never be alone. Just because a relationship has ended does not mean you are alone. God will never leave you nor forsake you.

"Be strong and of good courage, do not fear nor be afraid of them; for the Lord your God, He is the One who goes with you. He will not leave you nor forsake you." (Deuteronomy 31:6)

Don't be afraid to let your feelings and emotions out to God. Sometimes the shame and guilt we feel about our past can stop us from talking to God. You may feel like God is mad at you. These thoughts will prevent you from receiving His love and forgiveness. He loves you, and no matter what you've done, He's willing to forgive you. Hold on to Him, and He will comfort you and ease your pain.

There's a difference between being lonely and being alone. You may enjoy time spent alone without interruptions, the much-needed "me time" when you turn off the television or phone and read a book, relax, or even meditate. However, when you're lonely, you also have an emptiness inside, and that is what feels painful. Loneliness has nothing to do with being alone. You can be lonely while standing in a baseball stadium filled with 60,000 people. If you are experiencing loneliness, something must change on the inside in order for you to overcome it.

Mother Teresa said, "Loneliness and the feeling of being unwanted is the most terrible poverty." Don't get distracted by how things look currently in your life. This is a season, it's temporary, and you will get through this if you hold on to the power that is greater than what you see. Call on the God of the universe, and ask that His Holy Spirit be known in your heart. Get in touch with your passions and connect with the contentment and peace of just being you. When you were an infant, you were loved and cared for because you existed. You didn't have to be smart, rich or married to be loved. It may not feel like it, but this is still true. Learn to connect and be okay with just being. You have a greater purpose than what you see."

"There is a time for everything, and a season for every activity under the heavens:" –Ecclesiastes 3:1

Understand that your life is constantly changing and you are moving into new seasons of life. There is a season for you to build, plant and sow and a season for you to watch it grow. It's important that you understand your season and allow yourself to be flexible for the changes. It's not meant for you to build in every season; some seasons are designed for you to rest. Even God rested on the seventh day after creating the heavens and earth. Your season may feel foreign to you because things are different; that's normal. Embrace the differences as your new norm. It's time for you to let go of the past and everything that happened in your former season. That relationship in your past didn't work out, because the season for that relationship ended.

Say the following prayer and affirmations out loud.

## Miracles in Your Mouth Prayer:

Heavenly Father, I am committed to praise You and thank You even when I don't understand the trials of life. I understand that You are working everything together for my good. Thanks for allowing my setback to be a set up for your blessings in my life. I know that my story is still being written, and my hope is in You. Thank you for answering my prayers even in my pain. In Jesus' name I pray, amen.

## Miracles in Your Mouth Supplication, Affirmations:

God, I let go of all doubt, anger and resentment. I surrender my entire life to You. Have your way in me. I'm dedicated to trust You in the midst of all uncertainty. I declare your word in my life today;

- God is working together all the trials of life for my good
- My struggles serve a purpose to build my strength
- My setbacks are really a setup for me to be more than a conqueror through Christ
- God is elevating me to new levels in my life

- God is connecting me with new positive relationships
- I will no longer allow what's familiar to mess up what's better
- My life is constantly moving into new seasons, and I'm embracing the change
- I welcome the changes in my life as my new norm

**Miracles in Your Mouth Thankful Praise:**

- I am thankful for wisdom and strength
- I am thankful for God's grace to endure life trials
- I am thankful for new levels and seasons of life
- I am thankful for times of growth
- I am thankful for answered prayers

**Take Action:**

What will you commit to let go of from your past?

_____

_____

_____

_____

_____

## CHAPTER 6

## BE RENEWED; RECEIVE PROSPERITY AND INCREASE

God has so much in store for you. However, you must decide which reality will you live in—the reality of who you were in your past or the reality of who you are in Christ.

Everything from your past is over. Your childhood pain, the abandonment you experienced from your absent parent and the traumatic abuse you encountered is over. You don't owe your past anything. The old you passed away; you are now new.

"Therefore if any man be in Christ, he is a new creation: old things are passed away; behold, all things are become new." –2 Corinthians 5:17

You are no longer bound by your past. You don't have to explain your past anymore and the reasons you did what you did. You no longer have to feel guilty for it, and you definitely don't need to serve your past anymore. It's over. You no longer need to work hard to gain people's approval because of the rejection you felt from disappointing others in your past. You are free from it all. You no longer need to stress yourself out trying to prove you're good enough. Before you can really be free from your past, you must change.

"Blessed [fortunate, prosperous, and favored by God] is the man who does not walk in the counsel of the wicked [following their advice and example], Nor stand in the path of sinners, nor sit [down to rest] in the seat of scoffers (ridiculers)." –Psalm 1:1 (AMP)

**The Truth About Prosperity**

To live a blessed and prosperous life you must first change your company. If the people who are giving you guidance and advice are the same negative people you spend most of your time with, don't be surprised why your life isn't progressing. Who you hang around you become. Show me your friends, and I'll show you your future. How can you expect to be blessed when you're surrounded by people who are depressing? Be careful who you take advice from. Wise Godly counsel is your protection.

"Where there is no [wise, intelligent] guidance, the people fall [and go off course like a ship without a helm], but in the abundance of [wise and godly] counselors there is victory." –Proverbs 11:14

Over the years I've made a big effort to surround myself with Godly counsel. One of my spiritual mentors is an amazing woman who's about thirty years older than me, and her wisdom and guidance has helped me to elevate and grow in a balanced life. She tells me the truth even when it's not pleasant to hear, and the truth always sets me free. Change your company and watch your life change.

You become what you spend time doing. It's what you fill your time watching, readings and studying—that's what you become. Your mind becomes whatever you feed it.

"And be not conformed to this world: but be ye transformed by the renewing of your mind, that ye may prove what is that good, and acceptable, and perfect, will of God." –Romans 12:2

It's time that you stop feeding your mind with where you've been and start feeding your mind with where you're going. If you feed your mind with the things of this world (latest trends, depressing news and the scandals and racial disparities), you will always be moved emotionally, spiritually and physically as the world moves. You will limit yourself to the same habits and ways of the world.

If you were meant to be a butterfly but all your friends are worms, you will lower yourself to think, act and function like a worm for social acceptance. You may relate to their weakness, but that doesn't mean you need to take on their mindset.

God wants you to be renewed and to prosper and be in good health; therefore, you need to transform your mind. Change your atmosphere; pray for new divine relationships, connections and partnership. You can't just pray about it; you must take action and make room for the increase. You must be willing to give up some things before you can receive something greater.

Give up that toxic relationship if you want to receive a new, loving relationship. Give up your negative thinking if you want to receive the life results of Godly Kingdom thinking. Your problem has been that you've been getting too many urges from where you came from and nothing from where you're going. Make room for the increase. Get rid of all the blessing blockers in your life. The next level of your life will demand a new you. Stop running from the necessary change. Don't allow fear to hold you back from your future. You must be willing to elevate to the next level with courage. Let go of the old habits that have kept you in the same place. Transform your life by transforming your mind. Old ways won't open new doors. When you change your thinking, you will change where you're going.

You must position yourself to prosper. Everything alive in nature started with a seed. Any time something increases and grows, it starts as a seed. Every flower and tree started as a seed; every vegetable and fruit started as a seed; every animal, fish and bird came from a seed. You and I and every person living on the earth came from a seed call sperm. Sperm is derived from the Greek word (σπέρμα) sperma (meaning "seed"). Therefore, before you can prosper in any area of your life, you must be willing to sow a seed.

"But this I say, He which sows sparingly shall reap also sparingly; and he which sows bountifully shall reap also bountifully." –2 Corinthians 9:6-7

Prosperity receiving requires prosperity giving. If you want more love, give more love, and you will start receiving more love. If you want more wisdom and knowledge, start giving the wisdom and knowledge you have, and you will begin to increase in wisdom and knowledge. If you desire more genuine friendships, start being friendly to more people, and you will gain more friendships. If you desire peace of mind and spiritual growth, start praying for others and helping any way you can, and soon you'll forget about your problems and grow in peace. If you are struggling financially, start giving financially, as you can with a cheerful heart. Ask how you can make a difference and start doing something; after a while you'll see your life transform before your eyes. That's the power of prosperity.

You must understand that God's prosperity is much bigger than you. God's vision for prospering you starts with your seed. God is looking at your children's children.

God sees beyond you; He sees you as the generations to come. Your life has the power to impact nations. The blessing that God has for you you won't have room to receive. Your blessings are supposed to outlive you and pass down to your generations to come.

"A good man leaves an inheritance to his children's children, But the wealth of the sinner is stored up for the righteous." –Proverbs 13:22

**The Reason God Gives the Power to Gain Wealth**

Understand that prosperity goes beyond just money. You can be prosperous in your money, but true prosperity is not just about getting more money; true prosperity is about getting more wisdom and strategy. Having divine wisdom and strategy will guide you to increasing your money, but if you're only seeking more money with no strategy, that's poverty thinking.

When God prospers you in any area of your life, understand that is not just for your benefit but for you to benefit others. You are blessed to be a blessing. The reason God gives you the power the gain wealth is for you to advance the kingdom of God.

"And you shall remember the LORD your God, for it is He who gives you power to get wealth, that He may establish His covenant which He swore to your fathers, as it is this day." –Deuteronomy 8:18

"But seek first the kingdom of God and His righteousness, and all these things shall be added to you." – Matthew 6:33

As God sees you seeking to advance His kingdom first, then He increases everything else in your life. Prosperity is not just for you to wear fancy clothes, drive a luxury car and live in a mansion. If those are your motives, don't expect God to bless you with wealth. God gives prosperity to those He trusts. You must first prove that you are faithful.

"His lord said to him, 'Well done, good and faithful servant; you have been faithful over a few things, I will make you ruler over many things. Enter into the joy of your lord.'" –Matthew 25:23

Your path to prosperity includes the following steps:
1. Assess your situation. Where are you now, and what do you need? God said He will supply all your needs (Philippians 4:19). If you haven't assessed

your situation, you don't know what you need. If you don't know what you need, then you don't know what to ask for.
2. Identify where you're going. What are you trying to do? What are your goals? Write the vision and make it plain (Habakkuk 2:2).
3. Take inventory of what's required. Sit down and do the work required to understand exactly what it will take to accomplish the goal. Count up the cost (Luke 14:28).
4. Stay committed and never give up. As you diligently pursue it and stay firmly connected to God, you will be like a tree planted by the rivers of water that brings forth its fruit in due season; whatever you do will prosper (Psalm 1:3).

If you never step forward, you will always be in the same place. Make a conscious decision that you will keep moving forward. Go after the promises of God. Expand your mind to plan, strategize and think beyond the norm. It's time to do things differently.

Say the following prayer and affirmations out loud.

## Miracles in Your Mouth Prayer:

Heavenly Father, thank you for teaching me how to renew my mind through your word. I am committed to be transformed in every area of my life. I know You give the power to gain wealth. Thank you for blessing me and preparing me to prosper. In Jesus' name I pray, amen.

## Miracles in Your Mouth Supplication, Affirmations:

God, I let go of selfish motives and old habits that hinder my growth in You. Have your way in me. I declare your word in my life today;
- God has new blessings in store for my life
- I surround myself with positive people who edify me to prosper in my life
- I gain wisdom and insight from Godly mentors, teachers and counselors
- God is connecting me with divine relationships, new connections and partnerships

- I release all blessing blockers and make room for increase
- As I freely give abundantly I freely receive abundantly
- God has given me the power to gain wealth

**Miracles in Your Mouth Thankful Praise:**

- I am thankful for blessing me daily
- I am thankful for positive relationships
- I am thankful for Godly mentors and teachers
- I am thankful for giving the power to gain wealth
- I am thankful for teaching me to renew my mind

**Take Action:**

What specifically do you need to do to renew your mind?

_____

_____

_____

_____

_____

# CONCLUSION

No matter what battle you encounter in your life, always remember that God will never leave you nor forsake you. God will give you the strength to overcome every trial and challenge. Speak life over that situation. Don't complain or dwell on it by talking about it with others. Pray and give it to God. Whenever you think about it, speak God's word. Release the *Miracles in Your Mouth*.

Now I would like to ask you to do me a favor. Please share your review of this book online wherever you ordered it.

I also want to connect with you and hear about your story. Send me a testimony of how this book has blessed your life (contact@rainiehoward.com) along with a selfie of you with the book, including #RainieHoward and #MiraclesInYourMouth through social media @RainieHoward.

You can also find free resources and connect with me through my website, www.RainieHoward.com.

# ABOUT THE AUTHOR

Rainie Howard is a wife, mother and mentor. She has authored several books, including *Addicted To Pain and You Are Enough.* She is a sought-after speaker and founder of Sisters of Hope, an organization that promotes women's empowerment. Rainie's mission is to share the love of Christ with people who are hurting all over the world. She and her husband, Patrick Howard, are the founders of "RealLoveExist," a movement that promotes real love stories and healthy relationships, encouraging others to never give up on love.

To learn more, go to www.RealLoveExist.com

## ARE YOU ADDICTED TO A TOXIC LOVE?

The obsession of a toxic relationship can have the same enticement as drugs or alcohol. The pattern echoes time and time again: a new significant other draws you into a new relationship that starts off loving and alluring only to develop into a hurtful or abusive cycle. A person with a healthy understanding of "true love" does not tolerate this kind of pain. He or she will move on in search of a healthier bond. It's an unhealthy view on love that will rationalize toxic behavior and make another person cling to a relationship long after it should have ended. Like any other addiction, those hooked on toxic love have little or no control over excessive urges to text, call, manipulate or beg for love, attention and affection. They want help. They want to end the pain and recover, but it's just like trying to shake a drug habit.  Get your copy at http://bit.ly/AddictedToPain

**HAVE YOU BEEN TRAPPED IN A CONSTANT CYCLE OF TOXIC RELATIONSHIPS THAT HAVE YOU FRUSTRATED WITH YOUR LOVE LIFE?** Do you feel fear, insecurity and anxiety that has you asking yourself 'am I enough?'

You Are Enough takes readers on an incredible journey of self-understanding to explore the root causes of negative emotions that are projecting themselves into their outside relationships.

The concept that the fear of never finding true love and consistently trying to please others are major factors in engaging in toxic relationships. By addressing the fear and anxiety you feel inside, Rainie helps you discover your true self-worth, which is sure to change your life!

Get your copy at http://bit.ly/YouAreEnoughBook

## HAVE YOU BEEN PRAYING FOR A HUSBAND?

It's not easy being single, and when you have a vision to be married, it's challenging to patiently wait for the right one. It's important to understand that God has a divine purpose for your life and He wants to gift you with the right man. *When God Sent My Husband* is a single women's guide to gaining wisdom on:

- How to guard your heart yet freely love
- Preparing and positioning yourself to receive love
- Building a solid foundation that captures and keeps love

In this book, Rainie Howard shares her personal story of seeking love, dating and embracing the divine experience of God bringing her husband into her life. This is a miraculous story of God being the ultimate matchmaker. The book will encourage you to take a spiritual approach towards dating and preparing for marriage. Get your copy at http://bit.ly/WhenGodSentMyHusband

EVER FELT STUCK OR WEIGHTED DOWN BY THE PRESSURES OF LIFE?

No matter how hard you try, you just can't get unstuck. It's like sitting in a car, pushing down on the accelerator as hard as you can, and the car never moving. You are running in the race of life, but you're getting nowhere. Doors are constantly closing, opportunities are nowhere to be found, and you can't get your breakthrough. You've tried everything, but nothing seems to work. You are in desperate need of an "Undeniable Breakthrough!" Whether you need a breakthrough in your relationship, career, finances or health, this spiritual guide will give you all the life strategies needed to experience the blessings of an undeniable breakthrough. Get your copy at http://bit.ly/UndeniableBreakthrough

www.ingramcontent.com/pod-product-compliance
Lightning Source LLC
Chambersburg PA
CBHW071009080526
44587CB00015B/2401